Riding

on

a

Dream

by

Joyce Garrett-Williams

Photography by
Rick Benitez
Atlanta, Georgia

Cover Design by
Alpharetta Print
Alpharetta, Georgia

First Edition - Copyright 1999 by Joyce Garrett-Williams
Library of Congress Catalog Card Number: 99-94581
ISBN: 0-9672739-0-0
All rights reserved.

P.O. Box 189
Stone Mountain, GA 30086

i

INTRODUCTION

To a world of possibilities...
Is it possible to live, without stressing out almost daily? I ask myself. I chose a field of helping, good future, and job security. It turned into, a living nightmare. Over worked, and under paid, management didn't want to hear your complaints. Their attitude was to do the work, or resign. I found it increasingly hard to do a job, working for an organization, that could give a hoot about me. After doing the next best thing, job hopping, looking for the perfect job. I came to a very rude awakening, the whole system was crazy, it was a cover your butt mentality, dog eat dog, kind of place. Still loyal to this profession, my title will remain unnamed. The profession wasn't bad - just the greed of its organizers.

Many nights, I found myself frustrated, face in my hands, crying out to the Lord. Asking Him, if there was a better way of making a living for me. The only good, from being pressed so tightly, was I stayed in close communion with God. I prayed every chance I got. I would write my prayers to God, pages and pages at a time, when privacy was plural.

Asking God to reveal to me, my true calling it was very clear, I had chosen my field, not God! I knew when God was in the midst, there's peace, contentment, harmony, and a feeling of destiny. I quickly lost all of that, not necessarily in that order.

A small inner voice told me I was a writer, I thought, interesting... I would write about feelings, relationships, it was my voice, my therapy.

Early one morning, laying back on my sofa, closed my eyes, and asked God to help me with something unique to write about. To my surprise... He took me on a journey inside my mind; it was deep. It felt like a guided tour. We were looking at the different areas in the brain. The first area He showed me was the area of possibilities; it was the largest area of all. I touched facts of possibilities, I saw the solid mass of knowledge.

When we got to the area of reasoning, I took a seat and looked around for a few minutes. It was the most fascinating, it looked like a garden, it had lines drawn around. They mapped out what you could do. Then the little voice announced, it wasn't law, or how it had to be. Simply your ID, stating how He thinks it should be. Before leaving, I noticed a crevice. I said what's that? The voice said it was a tiny part of my brain, most common to me. I bumped into where my emotions laid, causing a tear to drop. I witnessed my mental block first hand... My eyes... Each time I opened my eyes to write these descriptions down, I couldn't see inside my brain anymore.

I was so elated with this experience, I just had to tell someone. So be sure to read my poem, "Mind Journey."

This book is dedicated
to the memory of
my late mother
Jennie L. Garrett
and her unlimited love.

TABLE OF CONTENTS

RIDING

ON

A

DREAM

RIDING ON A DREAM!

Inspiration, perspiration
    lots of midnight oil
I wake to it, bow my head to it
    it's deemed to be so
High striving, strategies...
    but it's just a dream .

What separates, elevates
    place the cream on the crop.
Is it something you're born with,
    to want to be on top?

Who holds back, launch the attack
    wise cracks behind your back
Hinder your dreams dull your beam
    break you down at the seams
All riding on a dream?

The young becomes the old
    unfilled dreams, are often told
Potent potential of times past
    how long will a memory last?

Looking through a looking glass
    fortune teller don't know
Hey you!
    Get off my mountain
    Get away from my dream.

It's not too high to climb over
It's not too wide to go around
It's not too late to attempt it
As long as breath, can be found.

3

How late... is late?
Time won't wait
   the sands seeping through
The hour glass
   riding on a dream...

This mystery slowly unfold
   taking shape from a dream
Visions from above
   delivered by the King
Jesus... is His name!

A gentle shake
   it's time to awake
   from riding on a dream
You've traveled this way
   day after day
Now you hold the key
   your dreams are for precision
While following the vision
   it's time to walk through the door

All revealed...
   while riding on a dream.

MOTHERS PAIN

Nine months you lived in me
Joy wrapped around each strain
Feeling your tiny twinges
Until you demanded
To be free

The threshold of death
Met face to face
Forces, blanket each breath
Millions trod before

Destitute in repeating
This infinite passage, some
Pain gripped, squeezing
Into darkness, seeing light
No more

Mothers pain, admits to life
The most cherished gift
Foundations mixed, nullify
Sensitive morals influence
No circumstances exactly
Fail through ignorance, yet
Obliterate poisoned minds
Of incipient zones inclined

Ripped out of mothers
Arms, weaned by spirits
Baring names, what?...
Has caused this breech

Prisons molesting our...
Sons and daughters

Crimes just or imagined

Once viewed through nursery
Windows now, crack houses
Trading goods for more
Until the grips of death
Feed at the morgue's table

Blood soaked streets
Screams muffled
With selfish desires
Fine grained caskets
With handles of gold
Soft lined velvety pads
With your babies
Head to hold

Lord have mercy
Much too late to snatch
Wedged in societies
Crack, mothers cry
For the children
Pray redemption...
Many refusing bended
Knee

You say your children
Are fine, college scholars
And success bound
Hallelujah for them...

But mothers pain
Effect all mankind
One way or thee other.

OH HOMELESS ONE

Not really homeless
Streets are my home
Natural resources, never
Alone, my home is where...
My house, a bridge under
Pass, a alley
A park.

Skies cathedral ceiling
Grass green carpet
Till winter will last,
We live free as air.

Trace the lines
Upon the faces
Disappointment, rejection
Locked out, of life...
Prized possessions in a push cart.

Destination, undetermined
But still I roam.
City lights, never sleep
Soup kitchen, where we meet.
System keeps changing
Justification defies
Atonement with nature.

Rebelling against chains
Of reason, declaring freedom
At every cost.
Death deceiving mortality
Lips sealed tight, caging
Words of regret, from

What was, equal beginnings
Until now. Hope racing
Against hope, praying
Endurance will count.

Statistics long ago, flipped
Numbers, odds the victor.
Still I roam
My home
The streets.

UNCONDITIONAL LOVE

Love a word often abused
Sliding off lips like vaseline.
Loves not weak, but resilient
Not blind, full of wishes
Hopes and desires.

Unconditional love
Conquerors all, loving because
Not if...

Love never fails
In a world of impostors,
Imitators of love
Confusing lust, comprehending
Not.

Loves a choice...
Seeking reciprocating
Recoil, flowing freely.
Long-suffering, saturates
Your soul, transpires
Mind, and body.

A absolute surrender
Of love.

CLOSE

So close
    I feel its velvety touch
Dissipate from my clutch
    Laid my eyes on it.
Smell the newness of it
    Savor its flavor.
I close my eyes
    And trace its silhouette
From memory's recall.

INSTITUTION
OF
SOCIETY

INSTITUTION OF SOCIETY

At the post office, the other day
Ms. lady in blue, hired to serve you
And... me, and.. Me and you.
Placed my money in her hand
Reached for my change,
Below it came. Slapped
On the counter, two thin dimes.

Almost forgot, I needed a stamp
She reached for my change...
We changed places, then faces
Omitted graces, indignity mirror,
Mirrored indignity.

Millennium on us and the confederate
Flag waving, like the good old days
Use the back door, still a nigga
Back of the bus, white only
Mentality, servant of satan..., if
A look cussed,
She cussed me.

Our sons, and daughters, cousins
And fathers. Dying of aids
And blades, guns, and crack
And heroin, like we have
Time to hate.

Cancer is eating us or we're eating it
Folk dropping like flock, dying for
The cure... go back to pure!

This institution of society

America the beautiful, land of
Free embracing remnants of what was
Left. And you say if you don't like it...
Go back to Africa!

How can we go back to an erased past?
What roots? Our family's tree diced
And scattered at sea.

Our forefathers beaten, shackled, killed
Our mothers, and sisters, raped!
Breeding your few minutes of pleasure
Stripping a nation of it's pure
Heritage, you say keep it pure...

It's too late for that, sperm soaked
The slave ships, and plantations over
300 years, we got your name.
We long stopped expecting 30 acres
And a mule, a liar's trues.

I don't have a family crest
I "still" don't know my name...

My soul annihilate fierce anger
Internal sorrow, remembrance
Of my ancestral dignity, past struggle
Through infinite spiritual recoil
Of God's sovereignty.

Death, simple, living perseverance
That took the bend out of my back.
Renewed strength to stand,
Not my might, He who lives in.

My soul should be angry...
He set it free. I don't need Prozac,
Lithium, Valium, Haldol, or Ritalin.
How do you sleep at night?

Lynching rope now invisible
Justice long due, racism, discrimination
Social indignities flow through veins great
Great, great, great grandchildren.
Word of advise, get it right...

For judgment day!!!

FRIENDS

You are a true friend
With unique qualities
And attributes, far above the rest.
Many have tried to be a friend
Many have failed the test.

I wish it were patented
Especially, for the world to see
The design of a friend
Just like you've been to me.

We've shared laughter and tears
Dreams and fears
You've been a shoulder to lean on
Ears to listen.

You don't see vulnerability, as weakness
Only as building points.
May this friendship continue to grow
More and more each day.

I hope you've found a friend in me
Like I've found in you.

GRANDMA ANNIE

Brushing Grandma's long gray hair
Twisting braids, and winding curls
While Grandma dozed
In a little girls world

Grandma awoke, with tangled hair
Reaching for, her little red can
Spitting, brown stuff in

Grandma would fish, at the lake
Sit for hours, she and her bait
Oh... She would yell
While drawing her line

I loved Grandma Annie
She was one of a kind
She would visit, riding the train
Big candy canes crowded her hand

She could have been a lawyer
A natural to defend
Saving butts, from mom's belt
Give 'em another chance

One day Grandma, came to her end
How could she leave us
At grandma's funeral
Her great-grand daughter, shouted...
All of these people
Here to see Grandma
She's laying there asleep
She really should get up
Laughter, through the pain

How do you explain
Grandma Annie won't be
Getting up again.

"ADMIRATION"

I'm beginning to understand him
yet I don't know him at all
my rapport, shared with thousands.
Oneness of spirit
common link, he's my joint heir.
Cool as winter's eve
showers of overflow
edifying to the mind.
Impermeable wall around him
crumbling, bit by bit.
I asked our father about him
his answer, eased my mind.
All things work together
many are called, few chosen.
This kind of admiration
truly is hard to describe.

THINK

Treasures
Hidden
Inside
Now
Known

CRITICISM

Insidious penetration
Malignant thoughts
Spread like wildfire
Head to toe scope
Meeting of eyes
Hissing surround sounds
Leaping
Mortal combat
Silent attack.

Life and death,
In the power of the tongue.
Should have, could have, would have
Lips that charm you
Suddenly harm you
Jogging lips, to open ears
Open lips, on bended knee.

If you don't have anything
Positive to say,
Don't say nothing.

And the world,
Was void of sound...

BENDING CONVERSATION
PAPER RELATIONS

You need a witness to verify
Each verb, noun, and adjective
That roll off your lips.

Natural bending abilities
From lips to ears
Leaping, spiraling turns
Make a gymnast envy
But, fear to learn.

Pacifiers bobbing up and down
Enfamil, and Carnation First Start
Fresh on the breath, of silverheads.
Spiritually crawling, and occasionally dead
Hanging around, to be breast-fed
No solids ever hurdled those lips
It would choke, and gag them
Just ask Heimlich.

Some hear, but don't comprehend
See, but reflect pseudo imagery
Infantile interpreters lurk, and wait
To dilute the truth
If the last breath it take
To put it plainly
They tell lies
Analyze that...

"MY CHILDREN"

Make wise decisions...
The decisions you make
Will last a life time

Hind sight is 20/20...
Keep your focus in sight
Do what's right
Protect...
Don't pollute your temple

Plan to succeed
Educate, and elevate your mind
Remove self limiting doubt
The only excuse for not succeeding
Is not trying again.

FIELD OF DIAMONDS

Mama tried to tell me,
I thought she didn't know
Save it for, your wedding day
Maturation know.

Who died and made him king,
And what universe she come from,
Have to blow cot webs off
Silently alone.

Boys lie about it
Dance a masquerade,
Through a field of diamonds
Few even view.

From mines in Africa
The hardest natural substance,
Colorless, tinted stones
To the highest bidder
Occlusions left alone.
In a field of diamonds clarity, cut,
And color distinguish the best.

Would you leave your diamonds
In a strangers care,
Wrap your legs around him
Hoping for a glare.

If you understood its value
A velvet pillow would hold it,
You'd guard it with care.
In a field of diamonds
Some things..., you don't share.

"STUCK IN THE MIDDLE,

FAR TOO LONG...

IT'S TIME TO RISE

TO THE TOP"

"STUCK IN THE MIDDLE, FAR TOO LONG...
IT'S TIME TO RISE TO THE TOP"

A man doing the best he can
Refuse, parallel of an infidel.
Desires higher, than rolled up sleeves
Priority strives, and feed his families need.

Assembly lines consumed our fathers
And clutched our brothers.
Diluted opportunities, and overtime
Twenty years on the line
Retirement with benefits
Dazzle young minds.
Uncle sam flying high
Crippling wings, blocking
Passage wanting to get by.

Laundry service cleaned another
Of creativity
Cleaning Ann's crystal chandeliers
And candelabras
Shining her silver servings for twenty four.
Barely enough energy to clear her own door
Sweet sleep, too heavy
For any dreams to lift
Dust to dawn, alarms trained to.

Yet another day
Stuck in the middle
Today, repeated yesterday
Yesterday precede tomorrow.
Same time, same dimes
Same faces in your spaces
Living your dreams

Above your lines.

Ms. BSA in her suit
High class, able to work looking
Cute, still in the middle
One step high
Close enough to feel it
Too tight to squeeze by.

Solid saturation, soak up the middle
Stagnant submission, natures inclination
Weakened by time.
Creatures of habit, follow
The leader, honor the teacher
Don't rock the boat cleaver.

A radical renegade, independent
Thinker, self determined, strong
Mind, unyielding persistence
Niche searcher, entrepreneur creator
Upset the balance of the middle.

Known as crazy, even lazy
Star gazing space floaters
Willing to try or die
Poetry of nature
Today's ingenious mind
Determines tomorrows
Rise to the top.

Sick and tired
Of being sick and tired.
Stuck in the middle far too long
It's time to rise to the top.

CAGED INSIDE OF TIME

Flushing remains of yesterday's waste
Springs forth, a new filling of
Caged possibilities, in its
Infancy, inside of time.

Long ago wanting to be free
Not knowing, time had
A cage of its own.
Mind's plotting,
Racing against
Its worthy opponent.

A time
A place
For everything.
Releasing everything in
Its abstract
Of time: it's whole, partial,
Or a season. Spans over
A second, a day, ten years,
Maybe a life time away.

MEDDLING WAYS

He gingerly pointed out
My obvious short comings
From his handbook of life,
Then turned, and strolled away.
As a deadman dangled
From his back, and fumes of toxic
Decay scented the place,
Like a plug in.

Through eyes loyal
Not to themselves. Spread
Deception like wild fire,
Burning out of control.
Half pass a dozen
Serving up lies
Like the U.S.A. Volleyball
Team. As the one mind,
Roll out of bounds.
Habitual meddlers,
Generative hierarchy
Sitting high, pointing
Curved fingers all of
The others pointing back.

YOU ARE A POSSIBILITY

You are a possibility!
a product of your mind
As a man thinketh, so is he.
we all know this famous bible quote.

What's on your mind?
thoughts are contagious
One thought, leads to another.
what you put into your mind,
determines what comes out.
Before you know it, you've
opened up your mind.

Explore...
the seat of conscious thoughts,
Reasoning, judgment
follow your emotions
They share a seat
in your brain.

MY GOD REIGN

I'm not here to defend
   my God...
I'm here to lift him
   up...

For ears, that will hear
   and eyes, willing to see.
I've allowed Him
   to live in me.

My Job's done
   in spreading the Word.
It's up to Him to deliver,
   and set free.

My God reign!!!...

A SINGLE RED LEAF

A single red leaf
Cascading from my mind
And then I awoke.

Reasoning was beginning
To shed, possibilities
Had caused, a gentle
Storm, upheaving in
It's midst.

A territory controlled
Of thoughts unprovoked
Magnetized, and aligned,
Intricate detailing.

Insurrection now in force
Healing wounds of years
Of neglect.

The scales, and debris
Flake from expansion.
A single red leaf
Compelled its stretch.

SOMEONE'S
QUEEN

SOMEONE'S QUEEN

Why does it upset you?
    that I'm someone's queen?
Deflecting my glory
    and slithering my glean.

You stand to take notice
    at eye bending, views.
While I stroll, sashay,
    and glide away.

A blood bath massacre
    is less conspicuous.
But you pray for sleet
    to cancel my parade.

Let me share a secret...

To be someone's queen
    no need of fuss!
Gentleness speaks
    and nature's curves
    a must.
A million tongues
    can't convince,
    you're really not equipped.
Weapons of war,
    tug against, a field
    of peace.

In tune with my king...
    I give purpose,
To his labor
    and joy, to his reign.

He adds sunshine
to darkness,
like coffee with cream.

We share oneness
in love. Division
all you breath.

Rehabilitation, might
be a way. Just
believe, you might
be someone's queen
some day!

ABOUT ADAM

Alone in his garden
Covered only by hair
God met Adam. Concerned
With the loneliness, he
Bared being alone
He needed a mate.

On a bed of leaves
He laid. He awaken
With Eve, his perfect
Mate.
Well...
Before her big mistake.

Brothers...
Don't be like Adam
Take spiritual control.
Authority over, to frame,
And mold.

Beware of serpents
And apples with holes.

TALK ABOUT ME

Talk about me
Just as much
As you please.

I am blessed...
Where much is
Given, much is
Required.

With all these blessings!
They've formed
A choir of liars.
Pissed, pitiful, and
Powerless debut.

My hedge of protection
An impermeable wall
With just a thought,
Could scatter them all.

Talking about me
Their biggest enjoyment
Of all.

KEEP GOING

Keep going, until
  I tell you to stop...

CHURCH GIRLS

Church girls
    control that passion!
Passing notes, down the pews
    soliciting thoughts, intended
    to amuse.

You hear the angels
    singing Diadem's chorus
    to the most high.

Fiery hot, burning
    just above both thighs.
Some gap, beckoning
    a cool breeze.
Young boys, clap
    and old men sneeze.

Holier than thou,
    mothers can't see.
Blind eyes, on
    kneeling pleads.

PRISONER, JUDGE AND GUARD

Bars of poverty,
    destitution, welfare
Can't erase.
    decoy, to subdue, gag
And bound. A script
    ordered to expedite
    matters.

Hasten the progress
    to debilitate, with
Detriment, to decipher
    worn, desensitized minds.

Hunger pangs beckoned
    each stamp to follow.
Stomach's demand will
    be answered.

Subconscious, judge deaf
    ears. Internal anger
Guard against, rejection,
    failures, and a multitude
    of declines.

A LINGERING SCENT
OF FORGOTTEN LOVE

A breath of him
    on memories bank, evoked
    thoughts of the past.
Buried under years
    of pavement, winding roads
    and atonement, miles from
    its origin.

His face, silhouette lay
    on the sides of memory.
That first embrace
    in trembling arms of
    innocence.

Forbidden love, protested
    canceled into futures
    worlds apart.
His laughter, residual
    around my inner ear
    echoing loud, and so
    clear.

Forbidden thoughts of
    lingering... dissipate.

EACH BREATH

Each breath, closer
To New Beginnings
Of effortless respire.
Intrinsic essential
Elements. Wasted
Like spilled milk,
Splashing to the
Floor.
Given to wanton
Ears, and then
Buried in the winds.
Tears refuse release,
None live without
Breath...
And no man die
Retaining it.

DIABOLICAL CONVERSATION

Clad in vile raiment
Shuffled his way over.
A face holding smugness
Like a tarnished trophy,
The solicitous approach
Produced squirmy under
Currents.

Slightly irritated, thrusting
Purposely into private
Space. A crafty voice
Of sour soil. Conversation
shifted, from soft to
A brash blasphemer
Against the Holy Ghost.

His dismal accounts
Crashing with the push
Of the wind. Mysteries
Stenciled on strolls,
Rearranged by a diabolical
Prince. Glory stolen
For his king.

An agile maneuver,
And released of eyes
Left me shivering
In summer.

MEMORY

Memory touch me gentle
Warm, joyous, hostile
Recalls ingrained.
Embellished high
Above reality.

Haunted by youth,
Memories manifestation
Of intensities influence.

Embroidered on life's
Fabrics, worn as
A quilt. Piecing
The old with the new
Good and bad. Overlapping,
Tucking rough edges
Of it's tattered pass.
Bright and colorful
Over shadows, dull
And dingy, contrasting
Victories, defeats.

CLIFF OF THOUGHT

Higher heights, and deeper depths
    ascending high as the hills
Surrounding the valley,
    so are my thoughts.

How deep is the forest?
    the depths of the sea,
Can you touch the horizons,
    or stand between raindrops?

Profound are my wishes
    of understanding.
Exhilarated, and anew,
    no longer frozen.

As heat rises to the top
    so are my thoughts.
Think not of me as dumb,
    in age, do we stop learning,
    or abandon our thoughts?

HIGH ON HOPE

I see those eyes
Looking, wondering
What I'm on. Standing
Close, sniffling like
Canines. Nostrils can't
Detect, high on hope.
It has a buoyancy
Of it's own.

Lapping as a deer
At a waters brook,
Quenching thirst.
Inhaling hope,
Feasting on its
Marrow, it's substance.

Stripping nutriment
By force, holding
On until change
Is tangible.

Stacking hope
On top of hope
On top of more hope.
Building, boosting
Exposing its panoramic
View...

Then sprinting,
Each stride filled
With pain, and its glory.
Wearing sweat, on my brow
As a crown.

TIMID GIANT

Tipping about tenderly, meek
and mild. While reservations
rest at the seat of his heart.
Afraid of his thunderous
rumble, quaking beneath.

One step would incapacitate,
crushing hindrance under his
feet. While placing insurmountable
heights, at fingers reach.

Swallowed by the enormous shadow
towering over head. Not quite
measuring up, not once has he lead.
His shadow overwhelmed him, reflecting
his image from a man's eye view.

Born a giant, not to intimidate,
but assurance in possessing the land.
Squeezed, tucked and secluded,
hiding inside of man.

EXTRAORDINARILY ORDINARY

Extraordinarily ordinary living
    from day to day, wondering
    of my purpose for being, created
In such a way. In God's image
    and in His likeness.

Why do some shine, like the North
    star, on a clear winter's night?
While others lack luster, or blend
    with the soil?

Their life appears to be carefree,
    trouble unable to find them.
But comes as daylight to dwell
    at my house, with suite case and key.

Have I strayed from God's purpose,
    blinded by the light? His hands
    not releasing triumphal rewards,
    nor granting defeats. Rapt in His
    wonder, lost in delight.

Painfully ordinary, but willing to
    make change, to stand and be a
    voice. In search of my purpose
Not just to be ordinary, but
    to be extraordinarily ordinary
    a mission, especially for me.

CALL YOUR LITTLE MIND
OFF OF ME...

Every time I feel it,
I drop to my knees
With uncontrollable
Laughter. It's more
Ticklish than the soles
Of my feet.

WITHIN HIS WINGS...

Soaring like an eagle
Velocity controlled in each
Stroke. Keen eyesight, avoiding
Danger, his powerful wings,
His cloak. A natural response
To shield, and protect what's dear.

Love's nest, where delicate
Emotions nestle, nurture, and grow.
No cage to contain it, self
Containment's within.
Understanding rules never spoken,
Audible with each stroke of the heart.

Within his wings...
Not just because he wants me there
It's the place I want to be...

NAKED

NAKED

Chapeau of deception
Concealed in it's dome.
Complexity resting with many lies rehearsed.
Pearls of parables, cultivated
Of times past, and prized diamonds,
Paid with blood, at body temperature.

Chains of bondage, clasp firmly shut,
Positioning around jugular's vein.
Deep piercing eyes, and tongues
Purely for fun. Feasting at pains
Table, until appetite's satisfied.
Searching for the next sacrificial lamb.

This coat is hot and heavy,
Who dare let it fall.
Exposing screams of shame,
Dark closets void of keyholes.
Bold colorful displays of coyness,
Gay laughter, silent cries,
Coiled roads abandoned in the night

Superficial sloughing of death,
Clinging to regenerated life
Smothering each new breath.

Destined to be naked.
Stripping in the presence of excepting eyes.
Quickly removing shirt and tie,
Track marks lead to a hidden past.
Buried beneath good works,
Changing tourniquet in to a tie.

But thank God, you're HIV-free
And gall will have you raise your fist.
To abuse your queen
Who stood at your side,
Praying you clean.

Girls young, even past the back
Side of young, standing in line.
One after another, bowing to the prince,
While he unzip innumerable times,
Not once mentioning that little drip.
Maybe if he'd remember your name.

Still trotting to add panties to this pile.
Breast exposed like a couple of young does
Blind by headlights.
Then lay wounded in the dark,
By a hit and run driver.

Even whoremongers, adulterers,
Murderous villains turn in for the night.
To homes drained of color,
With a thin glassy finish.

Bare in a field of vision,
Disrobed, with no hiding place.
Arms outstretched, just surrender
And submit to be searched.
You must become naked...
Before being covered completely.

80% PAIN AND GRIEF

80% pain and grief
   looking above, rain relief.
Sin and sufferings
   children of disobedience,
   turning deaf ears.

Tunnel vision, selective reasoning,
   hind sights always 20/20.
Even with blind sight you suffer,
   the same consequence, of ignorance
   transferred or inherited.

If I would have, could have,
   shouldn't have is too late.
Why me, if only, minutes late,
   now standing at hell's gates.
Asking, who in hell
   left these gates open?

Too late, to retract, and reclaim
   holy ground, and drift towards
   the bright light.

FREE YOUR MIND

Uninhibitable as air
Moving freely in, out,
And around the universe.

Be provoked of insanity's insidious call,
Lurking patiently, claiming its space.

Gracefully bobbing, twisting,
Dancing the waltz with her rake.
Laughing as it were her best friend.
People are passing by slowed to a stare.

Her long lean body
Life hadn't thrown any curves,
But her mind trapped,
Screaming silently,
Laughing with her rake.

War against famine-stricken minds,
Dying of thought,
Thirsty and hungry
Thinking is bread.

Rip off labels of delusions,
It's your dreams wanting to be fed.

There are forces, strategically aligned,
Causing imbalance, with a cluttered mind,
Fine lines divide / breaks of Reality.

HAIR

Kinky, curly, fine, straight
   thick, normal, thinning hair,
   designed for head covering.
So if it stands in protest,
   huddle in small groups,
   lay around lifeless, too weak to bend,
   or free in the wind,
   long flowing and loose.

As long as it covers, why all
   this abuse?
We call hair good,
   because of its obedience.
I give mind everything,
   it still falls out pouting.

Out in public acting stupid,
   not ever behaving, making me look bad!
So when we get home, I tie it tight.
   I just can't handle it, I call it a night.

Some people have the nerve
   to talk negatively, about your hair.
As long as they can handle theirs,
   why would they even care?

What ever it takes to make
   you feel your best.
The heck with negative people,
   let them spread fertilizer
   with all that mess.

If it means perming it, freezing curling,
finger waving it to your scalp.
Dying it, frying it, streaking, shaving it.
Girlfriend, I like buying it!
Take the tags off before wearing it.

Braiding, crocheting, weaving to
unbelievable heights.
Just don't forget to keep it tight!

CHERRIES IN THE WINTER

Firm and clinging
Unfallen from the tree.
Seasons shorten, by forbidden haste.
Grooming their fields
Calculating profits ahead.

Allurement of cherry pickers
Lift by the buckets,
Trees from its nursery,
Imperfectly complete.
Blushing, wholesome, fresh,
And bitterly sweet.

Cherries in winter,
Ripped from the stone,
Not allowed to ripen in season
And drop on its own.

WOUNDED

Rejection covered his face, like skin,
Dragging down his eyes,
Bowed his chin.
Shoulders rounded in submission
Out of breath from the fight,
Agreeing to loneliness
Holding him tight.

A look uncommon to men
Heart trampled, stomped and tossed aside.
Grooves downward each cheek,
From the weight of his tears.

Vain labor, years erased
At the whisk of a brush.
Memories cherished, out dated,
Out grown, lost in spring time
Unveiling of fools.

As the seasons change,
Sun burns, leaves fall,
Winter's chill, spring forth new love.

His eyes lift, like theater
Curtains post intermission.
A face barely recognizable
And full of promise.

Restored resplendence,
Two hearts beating in synchronized
Rhythm of the healing touch of love.

PERSPECTIVE

A call too late...
   words hang off vocal
Cords, delay need
   of their release.
Precious moments
   money can't buy
Given to waste...

Simple pleasures
   a hug and kiss
Or, I love you,
   the angle of a smile.
Quietness shared
   over cups of coffee,
Surprised picnics
   for two.

Intentions of
   another day
Planned,
   around time,
Each day,
   each moment
Of squandered
   time...

Pain, fuels
   the weeping heart...
Fragile
   this life,
When vigor
   dwindle to nothingness.

Angels escort the soul,
a shell of a temple
Lay cold, and calm.

Lusty tears cry out,
a call too late...
Compositions of life includes death,
vanishing out of view.

62

LICKING

AT

THE

SURFACE

LICKING AT THE SURFACE

Sweet savor filled the air
Tingling to the spine.
A quiver rolled across my chest,
Gently stroked my heart.

A hunger floods the soul
The feasting has just begun,
Not letting a morsel drop
Until you hold no more,
Overflowing saturation.

Tired of getting a lick
Of the Lord...
Licking at the surface.
You have to taste to see,
That the Lord is good.

He'll fill you until
You want no more.
Stop brushing up against Him,
Embrace Him boldly face-to-face,
And stop licking at the surface.

THE GIFT

Exquisitely wrapped
in a small, bright purple
shimmery iridescent box
And splashes of red, blue
and fuschia drops.

A big gold foiled ribbon
tied in a bow, cascading
down the sides.

Upon receiving the gift...
tugging, pulling, yanking
at the outer wrapping,
Anticipating its contents.

A diamond, gold or silver
precious none the less.
Pulling out the tissue stuffed inside
puzzled, just looking in an empty box.

It was the gift!!
that opened the box.

LONGING

Each fiber of my being reach,
Desirous of one touch.
Hope lacing despair,
Intertwining succulent struggles,
And cravings of past failures.

Crisscrossing, eclipsing rays of light.
A titillating thought,
Vibrate the senses,
And stimulate deep yearnings.

Unsupporting fears
Of unachievable triumphs,
But limitless latitude.

THE DREAM OF FATE

Late one night, long before day,
    fast asleep scenes flash in
    slow motion and technicolored.

I saw my aunt, my brother
    and sister boarding a plane.
Gloom sat on each shoulder,
    tears embrace, and roll off sides of cheeks,
    comforting each others grief.

My pillow grew wet,
    sleep held me still.
While family and friends
    met in a big church, lining the pews,
As Kleenex muffle cries,
    and wipe away mascara smudges.

The procession marched,
    starting from the back.
A shiny casket stretched out
    across the front of the sanctuary,
    in place of communion's table.

I looked down to view,
    oh my God...
My Mother's face!
    I woke up screaming, tears rolled.
I prayed like never before
    please God...
Don't let this dream come to pass.

Months went by, just before dawn,
    the phone rang.

Distress was calling!
Mom is dead!
The frantic voice delivered,
without a breath.
My mind didn't know
how to process,
So it froze for a moment.
Then Deja vu!

TODAY I REMEMBER

Today I remember...
Numbering all the days,
I last saw your face,
A smile years won't erase from memory.
I still hear your whispers,
Feel your tender hands of caring.

Today I understand
The lessons failed,
And why you refused
To give up teaching and preaching,
Using your rod of correction,
When nothing else reached.

Forcing my mouth to release
I'm sorry, even when they were lies.
You knew someday I'd remember,
And I'm sorry would have
A different meaning,
No longer forced.

I'm sorry you left silently!
When I said good night...
I didn't know I was saying
Good bye...

Nor, did you tell me,
When we said our I Love You,
Each sealed in our heart with a kiss.

I cherish the years you mold me,
And the pride you felt,
Knowing your work wasn't in vein.

Your love...
Lives in my heart.
Today I remember because
It's the day you left
For heaven's gates.

THE RUNNER

Trained to jog up warmth
   before a stretch.
Agility, strength and speed
   fine tuned, even in a state of rest.

Adrenalin pumps
   and primes the heart
The mind visualizes strategies
   like a chart.
Each muscle has their stretch,
   then summons for fluids,
   rest and diet to be put to the test.

When it's time to compete
   exposure is clear
   of the one's that cheat.

The starter's pistol pointed
   to the heavens!
Go with the smoke,
   and let the sound catch up.
High knees on the wings on the wind...
Bending with the curves...
And sprinting up the stretch...
Finish line in view, each strand
   of your hairs strength is
   put to the test...

The runner, determined to give
   not less than...
Their ultimate best!

SAPPHIRE

A brassy persona
And Rawness of naivete
Sprawled proudly.
But difficult viewing, on
Unprotected eyes of concern.
Cries of desperation,
Loneliness, altered self respect
In the sappiness of her breast.
The dipping of hips,
Skipping ego-trips
Weathering what comes, breaking
on impact. Agreeably without promise
Chain-react, improvising perspectives
Heartstrings strum off key.
Redirecting the swirls of the wind.

MY GREAT AUNT NANCY

When I was a little colored girl,
   with virgin plats and rubber bands,
Hand me down clothes altered to fit my needs.

Aunt Nancy loved telling stories
   about olden days,
When colored men, got beaten like slaves.

Her father was accused
   of some trumped-up charge
Dragged from his shack,
   and slaughtered at the flick of a wrist.
Witnessed through irrevocable eyes
   of somberness, mingled with the hot
Murky nights of summer.

Pointing to a hand of hatred to her mother,
   threating to slay the fetus in her womb,
If born a male child!
   If born a male child to die in his
Father's shadow.

Rage swollen throats,
   lips tighten like an anus.
Did they get them,
   killing your daddy like that?

No...
   but that baby born was your Grandma.

Aunt Nancy was a cool old girl,
   telling stories we needed to know

Chilling accounts of her world,
    of her past recorded on the pages
    of memory.
Just don't cross her respect
    life had taken all she'd let slip
    from her grasp.

She laid one husband still,
    with an iron frying pan,
And her hushed whispers of skills
    with lace and a blade.

Family lads knew her as Zoro,
    leaving Zzzzeees on their...

Her resilience baffling to children
    of civil rights, and near equal
Justice. She went to church
    sang hymns of Zion,
Till her dying day and left here
    loving like a saint.

TRANSPLANTED TRANSPLANT

The Ohio Valley enfold my folk,
Running from the South.
Solid minds of change and determination
To feel a new climate.

Northerners often read about
The world of the south,
Jim Crow laws, Ku Klux Klan,
And who with a heart could lynch a man,
And leave him dangling from a tree.

North restored dignity
Where colored folk were free,
And proud to be Americans.

The winds blow the snow drifts
Colder, then the Delta.
A one-way ticket to Hollywood,
And the bright lights casting its heat.

This was the place to be,
A city that never sleeps.
Making more money in a day,
Than some make in a week.

Life was a spinning top, whirling around,
Bouncing off walls,
Spinning and spinning,
But never stopped.

The moving van stacked,
With all we couldn't part.
Going back to a simpler world,

Gentler minds, where Magnolia trees
And Azaleas bloom, and
Dogwoods sweep the air.

YESTERDAY I READ
LANGSTON HUGHES POEM:
<u>THE NEGRO MOTHER</u>

It leaped off the pages
   from between the covers,
   and magnetized my heart and soul.
Resilient, steadfast, unmovable dreams
   envisioned by the negro mother.

Think not segregation!
   equality's not equally aligned
   for the dark-skinned children of this world.
Everyone knows our past,
   struggles and indignities.
Injustice of society,
   treating darkened skins,
   like the dirt they trod.

Times are better, but the illness
   of hatred's virulent droplets,
Infiltrate pockets of populations growth.

The strength of endurance
   from the negro mothers,
Embedded deep in their souls
   transferred in a seed.

Smuggled on cargo ships
   buried in the womb.
Underground railroads passage,
   through to the shining of light,
And promises of a better life.

Behind plantation out houses,
in pine boxes labeled "dead nigga."
Under bales of cotton
each breath made easier,
under-gird with visions of freedom.
Receiving trickles of safety, love and respect
due our historical mothers.

A negro woman
the colored women
Today's black mothers,
carry yesteryear's torch
Flames flickering high above
blood stained trees,
and shallow graves.

Prayers delayed, hasten
to the seeds, seed.
Prospering growth by leaps and bounds.

Her daughters learned their lessons well,
from Spelman's door,
Clark Atlanta, Morris Brown,
Florida A&M.
From Tuskegee Institute
to Central State Wilberforce.

Their lawyers, doctors, CEOs and nurses
promoting caring hands,
Educators elevating minds,
nursery care workers,
curdling the tiny hearts.
Clergies trained to stand in the gaps,
connecting minds, hearts, and souls.

MISSED

Rolling blue skies
Streaked with bouncy white clouds.
The sun sitting low on Destin's beach,
Waves clap, stand and bow,
Then roll back from its shore.

A gentle breeze wrapped
Around instinctively,
While sand clanged between each toe.
Sadness brushed against my heart,
Against my eyes, then leaned
Against my thoughts.

His hand wrapped around
A slender black girl,
Controlled at finger's tip,
Status, mute and power.

Padded men in cleats,
Dash across metered lines,
Off sides, unnecessary roughness
Penalized by a whistle.

WOMAN

Woman
A life,
Born out of a woman,
With the ability
To reproduce life,
Through infinity!

TIME IS WINDING DOWN

Time is winding down
To the final show down
Between good and evil!

LAURA

I study your grace
The slight tilt of your face,
And playfulness of your eyes.

The way you sashay wistfully,
Scattering dust beneath imperturbable days.

You share the beauty of simplicity,
A tranquil breeze off a window sill
Birds chirping in your lemon trees,
Butterflies landing on your screen.

GRANDPA HOGAN

Cool as a cucumber
Undisturbed in his leisure
Seasoned to taste
Savoir-faire like that
The earth quakes
Storms roll
Thunder claps
Gentle giant
Enchantingly naps!

REUNITE

Hearts instinctively reach,
    longing to connect again,
Seeing loves face
    unexpectedly in a crowd.

Perspiration drawn to surface
    anticipating words release,
Vacillate, holding back feelings
    standing ground,
Loyal to refusing betrayals of weakness
    and impressions of not being able to live
    without the other, even thou it's truth.

Dissolutions of reasons love failed,
    causing breech.
True love can't fail,
    so agreements are made to walk away!

Stubborn selfish desires
    satisfying ego,
While hearts lay broken in pieces,
    scared and defrauded.

DAY

AFTER

SUNDAY

DAY AFTER SUNDAY

Touching the tears
Brought on by the years
Touching the sorrows
Brought with living tomorrows
Touching life's grief,
The meat of your soul
Strengths you've earned
And test you've mold

Life is a test
You learn to pass
Struggles build endurance
As you go through
The tension push, pull
Stretching you to relief

Rewards won for yourself
And then to others to teach
This life we live
Not won by the swift,
But won by those that endure
Until thee end

To all of the young folk
Stirring up dust,
Spinning your wheels,
Omitting substance
But bathing in lust,
Of the all mighty dollar,
Idolatry!
The trend of today

Clinging to your bosom

Blocking God out!
God is a gentleman standing patiently,
Observing all you say or do

He loves you unconditionally
But Heaven and Hell is not about clout,
But the deeds of your journey,
And testimonies of your mouth

Invite Him in your heart to dwell
Getting iniquity out, not wavering
Between hot and cold,
Lukewarm he'll spew from his mouth

What will it profit you to gain
The whole world and lose your own soul?
This decision is personal
Aside from a group

Unless Hell is the place to reunite
For some hooping and hollering,
The crowd will be waving their hands
Like that, but this time they'll care

Flailing and fainting,
All because they didn't take heed
The same thing when Noah
Was telling the folk it's going to rain,
They laughed in his face until the floods came

We all know about the rainbow sign
God's promise he won't destroy
The Earth with water again...
But fire next time!

POEM OF LIFE

Life is the greatest poem of all,
   you're the composer of every verse,
Arrange them the way you want them to flow,
   the way you want them to fall.

You can erase, add or just blot out,
   dissecting rotten spots from the
   heart of your poem.

Some like frenzy, and living on the edge,
   heart's over pumping flooding the head,
Clouding judgment, living in a maze.
   some like verses to rhyme with reason,
Running down pages to a measure of time.
   Be it drama, erotic, metaphysical
   or fiction, the burdens on you to make it fit.

Poetic diction is a point of view,
   language without a license
A mirrored reflection of you.
   Expository, confessional, light,
   concrete, narrative, embellishments of truth,
   you are the poem and life's about you.

Parts of the poem we like best,
   we use as the chorus,
   over and over again.
Occasional lines jumble,
   crashing on the page,
   causing stress to break rhythm and rhyme
Just store it away in your memory
   of test, next time you'll know
   the ones causing mess.

Masculine, feminine, rich or poor,
all have the same power to put
poetry in motion shaping your dreams.

Look for the bright side
stop concentrating on the bleak,
Life is objective,
all of your heart's desires
won't come in a week.

We are students of poetry!
Scholars, educators, epic poets,
and drop outs, pastoral poets,
romantic, lyricist, as well as
tragic blood drained poems.

If you're unhappy with your poem,
write it down, make it plain,
this is your life to rearrange!

SHALLOW

Time spent flying
Too far off land searching
For treads, and envy of men.
Mirror, mirror on the wall
Tell me, which one will
Make them look like they crawl?

Dressed real nice, spotlessly clean
Mean as the devil's chilly reign.
Strolling, stepping, pimping by snubbing
The little man just wanting to say hi.

You would think!
Born with a silver spoon embedded in hand,
Heinously handsome or piously pretty,
With garden grown friends,
Plucked by the roots,
Arranged in a vase,
Each one knowing how to stay in place.

LEMONADE STAND

Gossip, criticism, backbiting,
Jealously by the bushels,
Gifts received for Christmas,
Thanksgiving, the Fourth of July,
And Just because they care!

Life has lemons!...
When all else fails
Make lemonade, Ice cold
Or slow brewed,
In assortments like this.

Grape gossip less twist
Non-criticized citrus
Blackberry back lick
Juicy juicy jealously free,
Artificially sweetened,
With no aftertaste.

SEEDS SOWN

Every action has results
   a simple law of life,
When unfavorable results surface,
    dissect and examine actions
    of the seeds sown.

A mean and nasty lady
    wondered why she had no friends.
All of the loving qualities
    of a voodoo queen.

Bars erected to keep love out,
    love no longer attempt
    to go to vixen's castle.

Gossip strangling it's victims by name,
    swarming the air like locust.
You dare to eat, afraid to speak,
    warring, keeping spirits out.

HIDDEN TREASURES

So far, I've found
Harsh, gentle, funny
Dreaded encounters,
Empowering, bitter
Sweet, victorious,
Defeated, triumphs
Self-determination
Plentiful, lack,
Successful plans
Freedom, choice
Life.
I'm still searching!

LAST

NO

MORE

LAST NO MORE

For years I talked
About success, school
Didn't prepare, working hard for a check
Never enough to savor,
Bewildering wealth, unquenchable.

Advise of miniscule rules
Prostrate before whispering
Campaigns of Wanton folk
Cheering for demise.

As Vena Cava empties
Theological virtues stood,
Vowing... to unselected love,
Self-pity pressed
Against a wailing wall
Drowning in tears.

Last no more...
Last no more...
The door firmly shut
No place for a key
Determination kicked it down
Last no more, for me.

If no road, I'll pave it
What you don't understand,
I'll tell you
Impossibilities my stumbling blocks,
Stacked one by one.

I use them as my platform
Stepping carefree.

The only thing holding back,
Is the air I breath
I say it loud
I say it clear
I won't be last
No more.

You might, ridicule me
I'll add it to, a poem
Like water off a duck's back
My passion, keeps on going
Adrenalin floods my heart.

There was a time,
Lack exemplified common place
And darkness, the only light I knew.
Gloomy days, and lonely nights
Gripping like a lover.

Last no more
Melancholy out the door
Last no more for me.

HERBAL HERITAGE

I'm a proud descendant of an herbal heritage.
Sweet fragrant lavender perfume
My roots and stems are above the ground.
Herbs and seeds collectively, green leaves,
Soft bark, from the motherland
Grounded into seasoning.

Without me would be no color
Without me substance is void
Without me life's flavor-free.

My anger blowing in the wind
Chains and shackles only of the mind.
Herbs are parts of the remedy.

My past is not whole
Convolution of cohabitance already unfold.
See the great beauty.
Bold colors
Unique textures
Patterns, large and small.

All apart of this herbal heritage of freedom.

VARICOLORED

Sky so blue
Breeze so clear
Grass so green
Trees so brown
Violets so purple
Roses so red
Hatred so gray
People so black, white,
Brown, yellow, tan
Blood so red
Life's so vigorous
Death so still
Enjoy all the colors
If you will.

PAPER RELEASE

Love, mixed sweet
Bitter highs, joyful lows
She feared fate

Reasons to stay
Clutched it's irony,
Fled hands that embrace
Refuse, gentleness

She danced with reasons
Love opposed hate
Optical illusions
Shadow boxing tears of remorse
Distant forces
Rebelled

Love...
Is what it does
Ambiguous touch
Pain radiate, each heart beat
No more skipping,
As times first
Eyes would meet

He whispers love
In deep pleats
Of frozen sheets
Scares of yester years
Orgasm can't erase

His love he never wasted
Touched by many
In hopes of loves' return

The cycle of many broken unions
Decreed by paper release.

IT'S NO WAY TO TREAT A KING

Soft darkened evening, no light for the king
    boys in blue openly in view
Sarcastic justice, long over due
    mouth opening, stomach grabbing,
Bringing audiences to their feet.

It's no way to treat a king

Video day view
    justice will know what to do
You stomp a bug, step over a flower
    walk around the grass
Boys in blue tried to Kill Rodney's ____.

It's no way to treat a king

Finally justice will prevail
    some will burn in hell
Pain pulsating movement lying still
    till justice
Upheld
    another ni__er
Evidence plainly, clearly, apparently
    seemingly
Not enough
    sacrificial lamb burning atonement
No place to call home

It's no way to treat a king

Know what I mean, just us
    opaque folk nil of the fuss
Tell me is it the 1990s or 1909?

Boys in white must have changed
the color to blue

ENDANGERED

Cheetah, running so fast,
Flesh-eating
Stops to rest beneath the brush
Journey city streets manhunt,
Like a safari jungle
Snakes slithering through grass
With man faces
Swallowing its prey whole.

Bloodshed, Mama's wailing
Through the night,
Like slaves running
Through open fields,
Laying low till morn's light.

Ku Klux Klan loves this plan,
Poisonous, self-hate, hunting your brother,
Negro-clear war
Atomic behavior,
Particle fall out.

Nullification of the mind,
Killing your own kind
Pseudo protective coloration
Alka Seltzer hearts dissolve in water.

Randomize blood, B+, O-, AB-, A+
Sickle cell anemia,
HIV tainted
Hemophiliac, Leukemia filled,
Hepatitis carried,
Cancerous shed

Plant flowers in this killing field,
Allow the fragrance to take control.

Dreams, blowing in the wind
Like pussy willow.
Bury guns, iron fortify vegetation.

Add my brothers and sisters
To the endangered List.
Hearts can heal,
Increase the peace.

VALENTINE'S DAY

Vacant was my heart
    until suddenly came... you
    echoes of happiness filled it,
    through and through
Abundance, an understatement, this
    elation took full view
    once I tried to shield, but it was fate...
    too much to contain, it kept seeping
    through
Love, more than just an emotion
    not just your tender embrace, you're
    my friend, my confidant, my knight in
Shining armor, with you there's
    a warm and special place...
Essence of life, our love has become
    as simple as breathing
Nurturing each other, to achieve our goals
    and fulfill life's purpose down the road
Time waits for no one, but love comes in time
Instinctively inborn, not afraid to give
    and receive love
Natural as the elements, bright like
    the sun
Everlasting, my love for you...
    is what has become
Still on the
Day we wed, two hearts beat as one
    exchanging our vows and rings
    symbolic as a circle
    continuous with no end...

TO LOVE

A

BLACK MAN

TO LOVE A BLACK MAN

To love a black man
Is to love a king,
From the beginning of time,
This was his reign.
I respect your abilities
To protect your domain
Sheltering, providing
Comfort and nurturing.

To love a black man
Don't come cheap,
Some are unaware of
The standards they must keep!
Dominance is a command
Don't accept defeat...

You must rise to the
Characteristic that prevails
"A black king"
Powerful, influential, superior,
Predominant is his name
Exercise control, integrity
And self respect.
With qualities like that
Who can't love a black man?

To love a black man
Start with loving yourself
Bundle up ill opinions, hatred,
Bitterness, and mistrust
Then... finally
Dust to dust.

Black men are strong, and striving
Tired of the struggles, they need to be
Loved and appreciated,
Not picked apart at the seams.
Tired of humiliation, viewed as crooks
Judged without being tried
Stop stepping on his pride.
The physical chains, and shackles are off...
You must break the strongholds of the mind!

How long have they been in line?
Yet overlooked!
Qualified, yet denied
Who are you?
To step on a brothers' dream
Predetermining his abilities to soar.
Give him the same chance
You give to Mr. Ivory White.

He don't want sympathy, just respect
Not a handout, but what's rightfully his
He don't want a welfare check,
To support his family.
He needs a job... better yet,
The opportunity to start his own business.
Not judging his business by the
Color of his skin, but the quality of his product.

Times are changing
And it's up to us,
To love a black man.
It's not a crime
Even if it was...
Arrest me!

LADY IN RED LACE

Extreme pivots, encircled the room
Graceful as fire
Ruby red lips, joyous hips
Sway back, stacked, heart attack

That lady in red lace
Whispers of manicured faces
Magnetized, void of pride
High heeled, nylon passion

Slow glance, missed chance
Fragrance captured illusions
Last wish, missed
Soaked in lust
Alone

Sultry solo
Hanging from a high note
Prayers ascend
Territorial chase within
Women cringe
Illuminated mystery
Enticing price...

SECRETS

Ask me no secrets, I'll tell you no lies
   remains eaten by maggots and flies
Devil had 'em do it...

Pondering the past
   enticing, betrayal, remorse can't erase

Dig 'em up... ashes, caskets, vaults, and tombs
   kick open... closets for views

Scattered as far, as the east is from the west
   the north from the south
   and the bottom of the sea

Fascination alluring
   like an armadillo, rolled up, grace his attack
Witch hunts, command a burn in hell
   the hunters, become the prey
Motives hasten repay
   he without secrets... dig 'em up

TO THE RHYTHM

Contemplation absorbed my mind
    as marching ants, across an apple core
His head pressed against the pillow tight,
    breathing to the rhythm.

The sound of moonlight, against my window
    pane, the stars marched, to the rhythm.
Ocean breeze, roll across its floor,
    crashing waves upon the shore,
Exploding to the rhythm.

Awake to the splendor, of the sunrise,
    gracing its horizon, slow dancing
    to the rhythm.

Swirling through the pearly gates,
    with the comfort of my breast,
The King alone, pulsate his throne
    climbing to the rhythm.

MY FRIEND

I've been trying to catch you so we can talk
    but you've been too busy
    and too hard to be caught.
Maybe when this letter reaches you,
    you'll return my call with a thought.

I woke you up this morning with my whispers
    of wind, and soft sounds of tumbling leaves
    just like you adore.
I then waited for your hello, but you rushed
    out the door, down the stairs to make
    a pot of coffee.

You sat for a moment, my Holy Word
    was on the table, but you reached
    for the daily newspaper instead.
You said you'll read with me tonight
    when you come home.

I waited all day hoping for just a soft word,
    when you were alone.
I watched as you drove through
    the dangerous streets covering you
    with my love and eliminating defeats.
You were about to say thanks for your
    safe trip home.
Your keys still in the door when an old friend
    phoned, you laughed and talked so long.
Still, I patiently waited till we could be alone.

I sent the sunset to slow down your day,
    sort of transition to end in a peaceful way.

You then got sleepy, but didn't kneel to pray.
   my feelings were saddened I wanted to talk
   to you many times today.

You layed your head on the pillow
   and drifted to sleep.
I tried to awaken you by shining
   in your eyes moonlight.
I then sent rain drops to tap on your
   window pane, you wouldn't awaken
   so I gave you this dream.

My love for you is as high as the heavens,
   as deep as the sea,
As wide as the earth,
   farther than the eye can see.
I'll continue to love you unconditionally!
I won't ever force you, I'll just wait and see
If you can find a little time for just you and me

   Your friend,
   Jesus

THE VIRTUOUS WOMAN

Who can find a virtuous woman?
Is she socially created?
Or birthed from the womb?
She's cultivated, motivated
Self-educated, predetermined.

She's short, tall, large and small
Jet black, milk chocolate
Lily white, creamy yellow
It's really not a gamble,
You'll know if she enters the room.

Ambiance precedes her
Beauty surpassed by deeper yearnings
Mankind and unity concerns her,
A refreshing change that lasts.
With gentle strength, stretch out her hands
Justice and loyalty are her praises.
An ornament of grace, shining like the sun.

Who can find a virtuous woman?
What sets her apart from the rest?
It's not meant to be a mystery,
Not even a test!

Her worth is far above rubies,
Your heart will safely trust her.
Satisfaction profits honor,
Delight increases confidence.
She walks securely in integrity
She's more than a precious jewel,
But a crown upon his head.

Who can find a virtuous woman?
One with the favor of God,
There are many, but few in between.
When you find a virtuous woman,
Indeed you've found a queen.

UNUSED VESSELS

Everyone
And,
Everything has purpose.
Every vessel its own
Unique quality,
No two identical.

No one
Without purpose, for existing.

Destiny, direction
Sometimes unclear.
Take time to meditate,
Get clear directions
For your life.

Life's a journey
Find your road...

Vessels used to its fullest capacity.
Simply awesome...
Viewed, and enjoyed by all.

PURPOSE

Life's first wet breath
    gasp, from dusty to pink
Eyes open to a blurry world
    submit oneness with the universe.

As years roll by,
    tug against purpose preconceived
Wearied mind,
    dictate shapes of thought
Stirring gifts, no more.

Frustrated and perplexed
    fragments wishes lay
    silence...
Often speaks to me
    even knows my name.
Reminds me of purpose
    ultimately...
Why life's breath
    flows freely and deliberate.

Oneness with God...
    and all mankind
Reflecting His glory
    awesomeness from the heavens to earth
Purpose...
    tells of His omnipotent power
    now and eternally.
To warn of the fiery darts
    and snare of treachery.

I might not have
    a millionaire's fate

But, riches beyond compare
    and a home prepared
Paved with streets of gold
    think it not a fairy tale
A mystery, yet unfold
    seek and you'll find
Ask... illumination is free
    everyone has...
Purpose.

LOOSE THAT WOMAN
AND LET HER GO!

Loose that woman and let her go
She's been bound far too long
Chains and shackles of the mind
It's time to make a change

Loose that woman and let her out
Your strength and power,
Towers tears to a deaf ear.
Loose that woman of her fears
Today and tomorrow years

Outstretched
Outstripped
Outworn
Occluded dreams, submerged in doubt.
Masked pain, shame, and disappointments.

Loose that woman and let her go
Rebuild, uplift, renew
Love smothered by life's struggles
One encouraging word
One warm embrace
One moment face-to-face

Loose that woman and let her go
Chosen to birth mankind
Her gentle strength
Designed to touch and shine
Freely...

A HOLLOW PLACE

Far from where, I've never been
   against my will
I wander aimlessly within
   silent screams, and dried tears
Fallen prayers, bounding around
   darkened air
Laughing out loud constrained
   few visit, willing its return

Inner thoughts, rage and wait
   sitting in a gaze.
Hoping for rain, for a float to the top
   the sun keeps shining,
But not in the hollow places.

Sunken without a trace
   eyes, all around
Not one down
   to the hollow of this place.

In a crowd, all alone,
   in my sleep, I still roam
A place I dare belong...

MIGHTY ONE

Give me eyes like an eagle
And vision to see the goal.
Ears fine tuned
So I can hear your calling.
Hands of precision
To do your exact will.
Give me feet like hinds feet
And the ability to climb.
Endow me with the strength of an eagle
With powerful wing span to soar
And weather the storms.
Saturate my spirit with your Holy Spirit
A reminder I'm not alone.
Use my tongue to speak your will,
And tell of your goodness.
Amplify your word in my heart,
And transpire your love in my actions.
Guide my will and way with your light of love,
Shining ever so bright,
Piercing through the night.
Alpha and Omega, the beginning and the end
El Shaddai, Elohim, all sufficient,
Powerful God and my greatest friend.

SONG OF SOLOMON

How beautiful are thy feet with shoes,
    o prince's daughter!
The joints of thy thighs are like jewels,
    the work of the hands
    of a cunning workman.

Thy navel is like a round goblet,
    which wanteth not liquor;
Thy belly is like an heap of wheat
    set about with lilies.
Thy two breasts are like two young roes
    that are twins.
Thy neck is as a tower of ivory
Thine eyes like the fishpools in Heshbon,
    by the gate of Bathrabbim;
Thy nose is as the tower of Lebanon
    which looketh toward Damascus.

Thine head upon thee is like carmel,
    and the hair of thine head like purple;
The king is held in the galleries.
How fair and how pleasant art thou,
    o love, for delights!

This thy stature is like to a palm tree,
    and thy breasts to clusters of grapes.
I said, I will go up to the palm tree,
      I will take hold of the boughs thereof;
      now also thy breasts shall be as clusters
      of the vine,
And the smell of thy nose like apples.

                 7:1-8

SONG OF SOLOMON

By night on my bed I sought Him
   whom my soul loveth:
   I sought him, but I found him not.
I will rise now, and go about the city
   in the streets, and in the broad ways
   I will seek him whom my soul loveth:
   I sought him, but I found him not.

The watchmen that go about the city found me:
   to whom I said,
      "Saw ye him whom my soul loveth?"

It was but a little that I passed from them,
   but I found him whom my soul loveth:
I held him, and would not let him go,
   until I had brought him into my
   mother's house, and into the chamber
   of her that conceived me.

3:1-4

SONG OF SOLOMON

Set me as a seal upon thine heart,
As a seal upon thine arm:
For love is strong as death;
Jealously is cruel as the grave:
The coals thereof are coals of fire,
Which hath a most vehement flame.

Many waters cannot quench love,
Neither can the floods drown it:
If a man would give all the substance
Of his house for love,
It would utterly be contemned.

8:6-7

I AM YOUR CHILD

I am your child
Love me...
I'm your instrument, bowed before you!
Play me...
I'm merely clay, you are the potter,
With your hands
Mold me, shape me, break me...
Mold me, shape me, break me...
Mold me, shape me, break me,
Till your work's done...
I want to be your temple
Live in me...
Your blood was shed for me
Cleanse me...
I was born an heir, and joint heir
Endow me...
I'm just a mustard seed!
Plant me, till me, water me...
Shine your sun on me
Lest I sprout not.
For all that I am, and what I hope to be
You give me vision, direction,
And many hopes for all of my tomorrows.

DAUGHTERS OF DISTINCTION

Yes, I am a daughter of distinction
what about you, you and you too?

We're not exactly the same,
but we are all alike.
When we learn to honor the differences
and appreciate the mix,
We're in harmony, united and complete.
unmistakably define!

Because we're strong, but gentle,
smart and still learning
Loving, giving, and forgiving
all at the same time

Daughters of distinction create and develop
motivates, educate and encourages
You, me and ours, or anybody

You radiate love and confidence
and hold successful, positive thoughts,
While continuing to pave the road for
sisterhood following.

Life is...
a mystery, unfold it
a journey, walk it
sometimes a joke, laugh at it
but it's precious, don't waste it
God is light, and daughters of distinction,
shine in it...

SUNDAY MORNING

Sunday morning, flying high
Thankful to the creator
This another day.
Death could have...
Made a home
His grace and mercy
Would not allow.
Honor in pressing
Wavering not.

Yet, cake make up cover
Streaming tears, wide brims
Barriers shade.
The great day of rest
Adorned...
For more prayers, and
Hopes of being called blessed.

This Sunday morning, my bed I lay perplexed...
Full of mixture, in my own heart I commune.
A miracle blessing, encircled my eyes
Enough to have changed many of lives
Fire fell, on my tongue
It laid, speaking a language
Unknown to me.

This blessing was a hoax
Not from above, not even for me.
Hard believing it was, yet harder
Believing intent... to deceive.

Fallen angel's
Squeeze my heart

Stunned my mind
Sadden thoughts...
Whispering if you're his own
Why so long?

God is sovereign
And cannot lie...
Whatever he promises
You'll receive, before you die.
The creator of time...
In, out, and around it, he dwell.

Not by sight, faith leads the way composed,
As this day ends.
Each day, and Sunday mornings I bow,
Giving thanks to thee.

ANOINT

Anoint my mind...
Of things more than temporal

Eyes...
Open to the hidden treasures,
Present and future

Mouth...
Allot words of wisdom
To edify and encourage

Ears...
Tuned, to hear your decree
And obedience to instructions

Hands...
To do your work
Lead, guide and follow freely

Feet...
To trod this traveling journey,
In this distant land

Spirit...
To guide the inner man
Comforting the soul

Dedicated to God...
My body, a living sacrifice,
Of clay to mold

I totally commit, my will, my all to thee
An avenue, for the master's plan...

Many are called, few are chosen.

WOMAN
GOD'S CREATION OF EXCELLENCE

From Adam's rib
  God's creation of woman
  would gently unfold
With his hands, shaping, sculpturing
  never using a mold

You are the essence of life
  chosen to birth mankind
From generation to generation
  continuing down the line
Great substance and integrity awarded to you
  hold your values high,
  no matter what others do
There's nothing you need,
  that faith can't provide
Keep your eyes on Jesus,
  let him be your guide

You were created to succeed
  and that's God's creed
Your excellence stands tall,
  and echoes the universe
Your strength is in your wisdom,
  and gentleness unrehearsed

Everyone has a purpose
  every woman her own unique qualities
No two are identical, profoundly prolific,
  reservingly refined
Some are similar,
  you're one-of-a-kind

Like diamonds in the rough,
  or jewels that shine
Share your divine inheritance
  Woman... God's creation of excellence.

TRUSTING IN YOU LORD

Trusting in you Lord, not in what I believe
    you can do or will do.
But trusting in you Lord to bring us through.

Trusting in you Lord, not allowing my fears
    to cancel out my faith.
Fear comes from doubting the power of you,
    and not really believing you can
    bring us through.

Trusting in you, Lord, when I see and don't
    understand and things I hear and not
    comprend, you are love no need to defend.

Trusting in you, Lord, you alone are my
    greatest expectation just to see you
    on the throne.
But while still here on this Earth I roam,
    thanks for your consolations of whispers
    assuring me I'm not alone.

Trusting in you, Lord, you've taught me
    to hope higher than hope love the strongest
    love, to believe in you a limitless God!
And allow my faith to smother life's fears.
    To lay my burdens at your feet.

Trusting in you, Lord,
    till victory's won over defeat.

Trusting in you, Lord, for
    my divine connection.

I will my life and all my possessions
Trusting in you Lord, and only you...

(dedicated to the memory of Gregory Garrett)

HELL

Mysteries of iniquity doth already
Work hidden, subtle underlying forces
Wide is its gate
The broadroads, most traveled
Walking after their lusts...

Youth and vanity, mask reality
Alluring entrance, with manifest tokens
Of unrighteousness...
Nations swept in a
Whirlpool's downward spiral,
Death cannot be satisfied, but gathereth

Springing forth contaminants
Of the world, twice dead
Without fruit,
Plucked by the roots...

Chained everlasting
Under darkness, flaming fire
Taking vengeance
Not quenched,
By a world of rivers...

Screams rest upon every mouth
There to receive it's own
Hell...
A place, you'll go unless...
You make other arrangements.

WHEN I NEEDED YOU MOST
(A LOVE SONG)

When I needed you most
You were right here by my side
When I needed you most,
You were my guide.

Covering me with your love,
And the comforts it provide.
When I needed you most,
You were right here by my side.

Every night soon turns to day.
You send rays of hope, shining my way.
How do I thank you?
My gift is small.
Take my heart, my all, in all.

I'll be your vessel, feel free to fill me.
When I was sick, it was you who healed me.
You raised me up for all to see.

When I need you most
By your stripes my healing was free.

I can't help but thank you,
In times of trouble, it was
You who vindicated me.
One more victory, you allotted me.
I'll always love you.
You've been right here,
When I needed you most.

When I needed you most
When I needed you most

In your love I could depend,
When I needed you most
I felt you holding me close,
And not letting me go
How do I thank you?

You send your sunshine
To brighten my days.
Even your birds sing
A melody of praise.

I have to stop, to say
You are an awesome God...
Omniscient, omnipresent
Alpha and Omega
The beginning, and thee end.

Jehovah Jireh, the God that provides.
You're eternal and changeless,
You're perfect peace, more than enough.

My all sufficient El Shaddai,
When I needed you most,
You whispered,
I'm right here inside.

GOD'S INSTRUMENT

I will go before you
And make the crooked places straight;
I will break in pieces the gates of bronze
And cut the bars of iron.
I will give you the treasures of darkness
And hidden riches of secret places
That you may know that I am the Lord...

Isaiah 45:2-3

FAITH

Faith is the substance of things hoped for,
The evidence of things not seen.
Faith is not knowing that God can,
But knowing that God will.
Without faith, it is impossible to please God.

MIND
JOURNEY

MIND JOURNEY

I closed my eyes ponderously
    to imagine, conceived.
My mind perambulate, not bound
    with laws of reason, but free.
Exploring spheres, no man has traveled
    then orbit, slowly around
Capturing, clear, and precise imagery.
This space was...
    my mind.

I touched facts, of possibilities
    firmly, in my grasp,
    this was the largest area of all.
The majority of my mind, untouched.
I traveled from lobe to lobe,
    landing on a solid mass of knowledge
    created by a much higher power,
    not of a college curriculum.

Weight has no bearing there,
    it's irrelevant, as time.
All movements, to the sound of thought,
    as deep as they came.

I sat in that area called reasoning
Much smaller than it appears,
    when seen with eyes of reality.
The only place there was to sit.
Vivid flowers, and lots of trees
    like a botanical garden.
Lines drawn all around,
    mapped out what could be!

To my surprise, this wasn't law, or...
How things had to be.
Simply your ID, speaking his opinion of how,
    he feels things should be.

Light inside was very dim,
    like walking on a country road,
    with the stars and moon, it's only light.
I was about to leave when I noticed,
    a crevice curiously.

It was the minute part of my mind,
    most common to me.

I bumped into, where my emotions laid.
A lonely tear, circled my eye with elation,
    of discovery.
I stared at my mental block,
    my eyes...
Each time I opened my eyes,
    free flowing from my mind, would stop.
They pointed out my boundaries,
    life had outlined for me.

The heater in my house came on,
    it's sound distracting me.
Forcing back to cognitive reality.
A place of limited possibilities...

Not knowing, what you can imagine... can be.
Those are the special effects of life, leaving us
    wondering how, it was conceived.

I battled my right temple demanding to ache.

Complaining, in need of more sleep,
resenting this early morning journey.

Utterly amazed of my mind's journey,
qualifying thoughts.
Challenge your mind, it will produce.
your answers rest at its surface.

EXPRESSIONS

No words spoken
Contentments on
The rim of his lips.
Sultry slits of brown eyes,
And a fire fighters mystique.

CAN'T LIVE WITHOUT YOU

Thoughts are cloudy
Mangled and confused,
Down trodden and deloused,
Ego ridden, guilt hidden
Can't you see, I can't live
Without you.
I can't live without you,
I've tried
I can't live... without you.

Life's a ball of confusion
Spinning beyond control
No shape
No form
Boundaries warped,
Dripping down fiery drains
Snagged on sifters edge

Knee deep, stuck!
Can't ignore
Hands reaching up,
Can't you see...
I can't live
Without you
Just can't!
Live without you.

Blind leading the blind,
Perpetuating 20/20
When vision has failed,
Covered under a veil
Pride won't admit
To glares blur.

I can't breath
I can't breath...
You withholding exhale,
You hold the exchange I need.
I live for you
I see through you
I draw each breath, from you...
Lord!

COMPREHENSION

Dawn's early morning,
Tranquil quietness of
Confusion, under
Pale, dark skies
Hovering over waves
Rolling inland off the horizon.

A fine dewy mist of ocean air,
Restore calm submission,
Atonement, in her belly cleanse,
Unifying, captivating eyes
Young and old,
Black and white
Inclusive of every hued shade of skin
Tanned, blended, cultured
Nationality under her
Cool, wet fingers.

Splashing, reaching until overbearing,
Touching nature in the midst
Of soaked sands, pebbles and
Scattered sea shells.

A radiant sunrise
Stretched upward streaking skies
Canceling darkness, inviting closeness,
An intimate touch
Toes dangling,
Dancing with waves,
Legs, thighs, slowly climbing,
Convincing of innocent
Intent of a wet embrace.

KIN

Sometimes you look
   puzzled, intrigued, disgusted
And unsure when our eyes meet
   in a crowded elevator, restaurant,
   park, or where the interstate forms
"Spaghetti Junction."

You take time to stare, examine
   and evaluate, quickly turning
   without a nodded gesture.

I'm your dark skinned cousin,
   your Daddy don't talk about
A splash of chocolate on the family crest
   landing in the shaft of your hair
Voluminous strands, plumpness
   of lips, dripping on hips, butts and thighs.

Too the rhythm of your feet
   swaying to the bongos' beat.
Swirls of vanilla a.k.a. high yellow,
   curly locks of blonde streaks
   and dark roots.

SOUL

Reminiscing the days whereupon
Men had soul
Blood covenants unified
Chain links of solidarity
Sequential of time-worn.

Intercessory leisure sacrificed,
Kids durst cruise
Beau geste uncontested darkness.
Rules cracked summons thick leather
Crossing cad backs,
Eclipsing ill resulted foresight
Renditions discerned.

Respect offered up ages ago,
Ceased hard words
From curb-sides release
Clear of offendable ears.
Preachers gleaned unreverenced souls
Unripe misbelievers, unrolled backsliders,
Misguiders, upheavers, fallen achievers.

Derelict meetings of dilapidated minds
Palmed cigarettes behind spirits
Camouflaged in brown paper bags.
Lodged in zones of comfort
Uncovering rebukes contritely pricked.
Promises of change lament
Tongue tasting lies,
Misremembering aforethought regale refute.

News briefs, muted cries
Shaded equality,

Editorialized by blind eyes
Outsized, flipped
With day ending script.

Prayers banned dispensers release
Schools sabotaged, camouflaged
Demoniacal theme incognito grandstand.
Bullets showering kids as prayers once hid!
Ricocheting off bowed uncovered heads.
Unaccustomed... victimized violence,
Random innocent blood shed and tears.

Meticulous madness hell-bent
Separating church and state.
Legislating rights of doom
To each and every classroom.
The voice of destruction
Heard loud and clear,
Loooud and clear!

How many must die?
Before reversal is near,
Erasing futures, shattering dreams.
Offended by prayer, is death an alternative...
On sinister walls of learning
The art of war, darkly illustrated
Memorized views, screams ingrained
Deep and wide.

Pray for the children
Pray safety as they learn
And against classmates snapping
Re-enacting Vietnam, encapsulating fear
Of perilous times, dropping at the sounds
Of doors slamming in cafeteria lines.

SEVENTEEN

A time when parents
Are unknowing, importance!
Self-centered the eye of concern.
Jump, bow, beckon every command,
Lest guilt riddled shame
Perched on your name.

Seventeen is supreme
One twirl of a wand
Life stands still,
Until endowment is granted
By the self appointed one.

Parents relax,
This too shall pass.
Pray that eighteen
Is closer to reality!

To My Big brother,
Ronald A. Garrett

One of the few stallions
Unbridled to life's
Prefabricated molds,
Some spirits roam free!

NAMES OF GOD

Elohim: Describes God's greatness and glory: it displays God's power and sovereignty. His unimaginable power involved in the force of creativity which cause our vast universe to exist.

Jehovah: The revealing one; reveals himself as your intimate and personal God. The more you grow in Him, the more of himself He will reveal to you. Jehovah the unchangeability of God. The God of life, the God of eternity.

El Shaddai: He who is all sufficient; God is more than enough to meet your needs in each situation. The God who is all sufficient will bless you and multiply you. He will work contrary to nature to overcome any difficult circumstances. He is the God of abundance and prosperity.

Adonai: Reflects our responsibility as his servants. This name signifies ownership and our own responsibilities that comes from being owned by God **Adonai Master**.

Jehovah Jireh: He is eternal and changeless, he is a God of righteousness and holiness. He desires to meet your needs, he's the God that provides... God has seen ahead and made a provision to fill your need, he's your perfect provision.

Jehovah M'Kaddesh: Jehovah who sanctifies, one who desires to set you apart by making your personality one with His. He is the holy one who demands holiness from his children.

Jehovah Nissi: You must see yourself as being only in Him. For without Him, you can do nothing, but with Him, all things are possible. Jehovah Nissi means Jehovah my banner. He is your protection.

Jehovah Rophe: Means Jehovah heals, the lord your health. Jesus heals those with emotional wounds, the broken-hearted and physical afflicted, backsliding and sin. He is health in every area of life.

Jehovah Shalom: Has exactly what the world is looking for, *perfect peace.* Peace comes because of he who is inside you. Be careful for nothing, but in everything by prayer and supplication with Thanksgiving let your request be made known unto God. And the peace of God which passeth all understanding, shall keep your hearts and minds through Christ Jesus.

Jehovah Tsidkenu: Means Jehovah our righteousness. Thy righteousness is an everlasting righteousness, and thy law is the truth. The righteousness of thy testimonies is ever-lasting.

Jehovah Rohi: Jehovah my shepherd feeds his flock according to the integrity of his heart. You can discern a false shepherd by being aware of the qualities of a true shepherd. He's

155

the still small voice, the word inside you.
That's how he guides you.

Jehovah Elohay: A very personal God, the one
on whom we call when we need a miracle and
know that He will work in our behalf to bring
us victory and success.

ACKNOWLEDGMENTS

To God, the owner of my life, from inception through eternity. His hands stretched out, cradling me in His palms, placed in me a free will. After flying through distant arenas, the good times, and vanities of my youth. His unconditional love, grace, and mercy would woo me. His hands remained open, awaiting my return, from the day I landed back into His palms, I vowed to live my life... In His hands. Thanks to the Holy Spirit, the messenger, for letting me know the will of God for my life.

Special thanks to Edward Williams Sr., for being my best friend, husband and soulmate forever. Always a gentle heart. Thanks for sharing love, whole and barrier free in confidence and security. I walk a little taller, smile a bit brighter when you're around, a breath of morning air, pure and simple, the boy in you brings out the girl in me; I wear your love like a blanket. He's encouraged me to write and to stop worrying about folks... some battles you shouldn't fight!

I would be amiss, in not acknowledging the fireworks in my life, never a dull moment. My darling daughter Keeyonna Hogan, and finally my friend getting ready to take the world by storm. To Austin Hogan, my devoted son, a credit to society, and the world of U.S.A Track & Field, thanks for always being my faithful audience.

To my pastor, Wiley Jackson, Jr., for the many sermons on faith, he's imparted in my heart. Especially the ones that caused me to put the Word in action. His lovely wife Mary, and her boldness in loving God, instructing us to draw from our heavenly bank account.

To the warriors, Karen Hines, and Marchell Brown. Thanks for covering, and speaking encouragement to doubt, pointing out the legs of a dream.

Charles and Pam McKinnie, an epitome of life's rare finds, I am honored to have you guys as our friends. Gene and Juliet Cotton, a class of their own, and a living witness that there's nothing too big for God.

Sonya Brazell, my only sister, bask in His presence. It's only just begun, all my love unconditional.